ISIS, HEZBOLLAH, HAMAS AND Al QAEDA –

THE VISION THAT WILL CAST DISASTER UPON YOU

‖‖‖ ‖ ‖‖‖‖‖‖‖‖ ‖‖ ‖ ‖‖‖‖ ‖‖‖
I0420315

RADICAL ISLAM -
WHAT THEY DON`T WANT YOU TO KNOW

Credit for background image: dominic lockyer | Flicker

Tel: 97254-8030648

Email: kobimnsil@gmail.com

Website: www.kobisha.com

CLARIFICATION

A fierce war is going on in the Middle East. This is not a new war but a direct continuation of the war that has been going on for over 1,300 years between the Sunnis and the Shiites. To a Western person these terms do not mean much but actually their meaning is crucial to Western civilization as well as to other civilizations and in fact this is a global war without borders as we know them.

During the 20s national states popped up across the Middle East: Iraq, Jordan, Syria, Lebanon, Libya etc. This nationalism was in fact a sham, the result of Western utopia. Beneath the surface the same ancient forces have been bubbling awaiting their finest hour for a breakthrough. This breakthrough became possible due to the weakening of the Western powers lead by the USA. These forces, that are far more ancient than most Western countries, are insatiable and interpret appeasement, conciliation and compromise as a weakness. These forces have a clear concept about the future of mankind and they are not fighting over some territory but over imposing an uncompromising messianic religious ideology. The essence of this war is to spread like wildfire all over the globe. Its first signs have already emerged in Europe and we are only at the threshold of the messianic - Islamic Renaissance. I think that every person should read this book and understand the true motivations behind the fierce and endless battles that will accompany us in the next few decades. I do not mean to sound dramatic, only practical.

By nature of my being a resident in this neighborhood of the world I included in many examples the implications of the radical Islamic activity in Israel while the inference is in fact much wider and includes Western people. As I emphasize in all my books – I most definitely do not try to tilt   the truth, I do not try to manipulate; in this book I present the simple truth for you to judge.

ABOUT THE AUTHOR

Kobi Shashoua is an author and a lecturer. Among his books you can find the most comprehensive book that is available to date about the Israeli-Palestinian conflict "Israel: the truth, the whole truth and nothing but the truth." This book leads the reader chapter by chapter through the complex reality of the conflict and dissects the causes for the crisis, uncovers to the reader the true faces of the parties involved, and presents the tactics, the strategies and the true objectives, that lie below the surface. The author also wrote the book series: "Understanding the Middle East". The book you are holding in your hands is from that series.

The author, who resides in Israel, located in the most dangerous neighborhood of the world in the heart of the Middle East, shares with us the facts together with the insights and the unique understanding of the region where he lives. We welcome you to take part in this journey from a safe distance.

TABLE OF CONTENTS

- They don't want you to know what is broadcasted on the Palestinian TV.

- They don't want you to know: everyone is a Palestinian.

- They don't want you to know what the political platform of the Hamas is.

- They don't want you to know: there is an Islamic imperialism.

- They don't want you to know: the goal of Islam is to rule the world.

- What are the Sharia laws that will apply once the Islam gains control over the world?

- They don't want you to know that as far as they are concerned all of you are heretics: you are
   next in line!

- When talking about occupied territories, does it mean also Spain?

FOREWORD

The purpose of this book is to shatter some firmly entrenched views that are considered by most readers as the truth. It is possible to write many books on each subject in the book. My aim is not to weary the reader with many details and subtleties but to present the main things in a clear and fluent language and therefore I will discuss briefly many topics that have in common the disinformation that is transmitted and the concealed agenda that are a threat to modern life.

Sometimes I may begin with issues that do not always correlate directly to each other, but they are all connected to the subject of the chapter namely what, after all, is the truth "that they don`t want you to know". This was well described by a phrase from the old series "The X-Files":   "The truth is out there".

We shall place the truth against the myths that are related to it, and we shall see how years of brainwashing, superficiality and media cooperation, have created a parallel universe that has no connection or grasp in reality. Its entire existence becomes possible due to its acceptance as an absolute truth in the minds of people.

The truth is always the truth, even if there are attempts to bury or sweep it, even if it ceases to exist in the minds of people. The truth continues to exist, it is waiting for an opportune moment to be revealed, like the truth in this book. So let`s go ahead and hit the road:

- They don`t want you to know: how many Muslims have been killed by Muslims.

Let us check and examine what is the significance of the victims in the Middle Eastern conflict out of the total of Muslim victims, how many Muslims have been "slaughtered" by the "despicable Zionists" out of the total Muslims who have been killed.

Did you know: the Al-Qaeda organization[1] has killed eight times more Muslims than non-Muslims.

Between the years 2004-2008, the Al-Qaeda terror organization assumed responsibility for 313 attacks that caused the death of 3010 people. Some of the attacks were carried out in Western territories as well, such as the terrorist attack in Madrid in 2004 and in London in 2005.

---

[1] A reminder: Al-Qaeda or in its nickname "The World Islamic Front for fighting Crusaders and Jews" – is a Sunni Islamist Islamic global terror organization, founded by the Palestinian terrorist Abdullah Azzam in 1988, and has been operating under the leadership and the financing of the Saudi terrorist Osama Bin Laden until his assassination in the Neptune`s Spear operation in 2011. The organization carried out murderous and destructive terror attacks that caused the death and injury of thousands of people around the world and mainly in the USA including the 9/11 Twin Towers attack. This terror organization is considered sophisticated and cruel, it strikes intentionally and indiscriminately children, women and elderly people, as well as holy sites of different religions.
From Wikipedia under "Al-Qaeda".

Nevertheless, only 12% (371) of the dead were Westerners. [2]

While it seems that the Middle East conflict leads to "a brutal genocide of the Palestinians", fierce wars with millions of deaths are and have been fought unhindered far from the spotlight. What does that mean? In an article published by the journalists Gunnar Heinsohn and Daniel Pipes on October 8th 2008 [3] in the magazine

Frontpagemag.com, the researchers presented the following findings [4]:

Out of the 85 million victims from all the nations in the various wars that have been going on since 1948, 35 thousands Muslims were killed as a result of the Israeli-Arab conflict and about 16,000 Israelis (let's remember that the number of Jews is about 13 million, while the number of Muslims is over one and a half billion).

It turns out that the proportion of deaths in the conflict out of all the deaths is 0.04%.

MAKES NO SENSE!

I mentioned this because the Israeli-Palestinian conflict is perceived by many as the primary conflict today, and therefore Israel is perceived as a belligerent state.

And what about the number of Muslims that got killed?

The article continues and emphasizes that out of 11,000,000 Muslims that have been killed since 1948, 35,000 were killed as a result of the uncompromising war against Israel. Namely, 0.3% of the Muslims!

I emphasize again: according to the article, for every Muslim that was killed as a result of the Israeli-Arab conflict, 315 Muslims were massacred by their brothers! Rough estimates add to these numbers about 400,000 Muslims that have been massacred since the outbreak of the "Arab Spring" revolution on December 2011 and the end is not yet in sight.

Would you have believed that over 10 million Muslims have been massacred by Muslims!

MAKES NO SENSE!

(2) http://www.spiegel.de/international/world/0,1518,660619,00.html/

Note that this is about terrorist attacks that Al-Qaeda took responsibility for.

(3) And this is still prior to the "Arabic spring" that adds another hundreds of thousands or even million to the number of Muslims slaughtered by their brothers.

(4) http://archive.frontpagemag.com/readArticle.aspx?ARTID=28394

- They don`t want you to know: the truth about the humanitarian crisis in the Gaza Strip.

We became acquainted with this crisis during the Turkish "Peace Flotilla", which transported supplies and equipment to the besieged Gaza Strip in May 2010. Since then, and regardless of the endless violence that is raging all over the world, aid flotillas go out to the Gaza Strip.

Superficially, it seems that many people in Gaza are starving and that the food crisis is very serious and dwarfs the food crisis in Africa. The impression is that the siege and the isolation are so horrible, that peace activists all over the world are relinquishing their wish to contribute to the African continent, to promote human rights and women`s rights in Iran or, God forbid, help the miserable Syrian people hundreds of thousands of whom are massacred in the name of religion and in many countries, and even to help break the siege imposed on North Korea and on the starving population there at that time.

Logically, in a place where there is shortage in basic things such as food and medicines, there is low life expectancy. In a place where there is hunger, it is likely that life expectancy will be lower. In Africa, for example, the average life expectancy is between 50 to 60 years.

But if we check the life expectancy of the residents of the Gaza Strip, we will rub our eyes in disbelief. Let's look at the data: life expectancy of Gaza residents in 2014 was 74.64 [5]. On the other hand, life expectancy of the citizens of its southern neighbor, Egypt, was 73.45. Life expectancy in Iran is 70.89. In Turkey, that is so eager to ease a bit the hunger suffered by the Palestinians who live in the Gaza Strip, life expectancy is lower 73.29 years

(It seems that the right thing to do is to send from the Gaza Strip to Turkey aid flotillas with equipment and medicines, in order to increase the life expectancy of the Turks).

(5) From the CIA website

In a place where there is a humanitarian crisis, we will expect to see empty markets with no goods but with long queues lining up for food.

People living in a humanitarian crisis do not reach such longevity. This is how a population in a humanitarian crisis looks like:

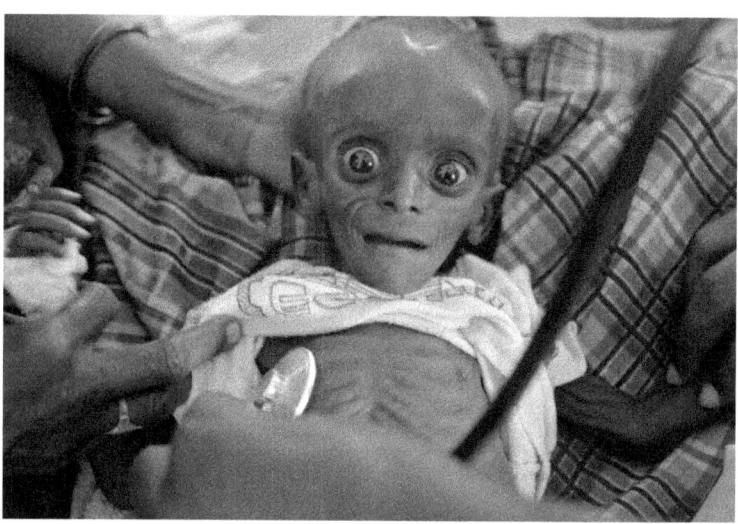

A doctor examines Minhaj Gedi Farah, a seven-month-old child with a weight of 3.4kg, in a field hospital of the International Rescue Committee, IRC, in the town of Dadaab, Kenya (26.07.11) / AP Archive.

But who really cares? It is in Africa.

The humanitarian crisis in the Gaza Strip can be summarized as follows:

You want to see more? Look for the set "Gaza good life"[6] on *flickr*.

---

[6] By proisraeli

- *FREE GAZA* – they don`t want you to know: Israel withdrew from Gaza in 2005.

FREE GAZA is a slogan recited by peace activists from all over the world.

*Flicker/ Takver

The Gaza Strip should be freed immediately. I also agree with this statement. Gaza should be freed. But from whom actually? From Israel?

Israel withdrew unilaterally from the Gaza Strip in 2005. No Jew or Zionist remained in the Gaza Strip. If the meaning of the above slogan is to liberate Gaza from Israel: Gaza has been liberated from Israel - mission accomplished.

However, ever since the withdrawal of Israel from the Gaza Strip, the strip has turned into the front stronghold of radical Islam, controlled by the Hamas organization that upholds (according to its platform) the following principle: "Judgment day will not arrive until the Muslims fight the Jews, and when the Jew will hide behind rocks and trees the rocks and the trees will say, "Oh Muslim, oh servant of Allah, there is a Jew behind me, come and kill him". [7]

In addition, ever since the Gaza Strip was "liberated" from Israel, it has been doing everything to try and penetrate the border into Israel. The Gaza Strip borders with Egypt, and Egypt as well has closed its borders. Why ask Israel to open its border to a hostile population? A population led by a government that calls for the destruction of Israel and that is defined as a terror organization?

----

[7] Hamas treaty, article 7

Why not open, for instance, the border between North Korea and South Korea? Why not wait to see how that works, and then open the borders here.

- Economists: The Euro-zone is in danger – Islam will conquer Europe.

Not only economists warn about it, but also I. I do not warn by virtue of my being a financier, but from a rather completely different aspect.

The Center for Economics and Business Research in Britain predicts that the Euro will not survive in the next decade.

Beyond the preoccupation with the question whether the Euro will manage to survive the swelling debt crisis in Europe, there is another question. Will Europe remain Europe in the coming decades or will it change its character? The identity of the countries in Europe has been formed for thousands of years. Empires rose, ruled for centuries, fell, and were replaced by others.

Today, a non-industrial revolution is occurring in Europe. A quiet revolution (though not really so today) that will change the face of Europe forever.

In order to maintain the size of the population, the fertility rate of each woman should be 2.1 children. The European data indicate the shrinkage of the population and its aging. The productivity rate in 2013 was 1.55 children per woman. [8] Immigrants from the former colonies and from Muslim countries came to the aid of aging and spoiled Europe in order to fill in the deficiency. They arrive in quantities and their rate of reproduction is enviable.

As of 2010 (unfortunately I could not get more accurate information – I wonder why?!) it is estimated that in Amsterdam, Brussels and Marseille between 20% and 25% of the population are Muslims. In Birmingham, Cologne, Copenhagen, Leicester, London, Paris, Rotterdam, Stockholm, Strasbourg and Hague, the Muslim population is estimated between10%-20%. In Antwerp, Berlin, Hamburg and Vienna, the Muslim population is estimated between 5%-10%[9].

---

(8)http://epp.eurostat.ec.europa.eu/tgm/table.do?tab=table&init=1&language=en&pcode=tsdde220&plugin=0

(9) http://www.hudson-ny.org/1536/islam-religion-of-europe, Will Islam Become the Religion of Europe? by Soeren Kern, September 9, 2010

And now a quiz:

What is the most widespread name for babies that are born in Britain?

1. Harry
2. Jack
3. James
4. Muhammad

Today, the most widespread name for babies that are born in Britain is Muhammad, not Harry and not Jack, but simply Mohammad and its derivatives.[10]

MAKES NO SENSE!

Luckily there is another authority who expressed himself on the subject:
The Libyan ruler, rest in peace, the dictator Gaddafi, predicted the future of Europe: "We have 50 million Muslims in Europe. There are signs that Allah destined the victory of Islam to be without swords, without guns, without campaigns of conquest. The 50 million Muslims in Europe will turn it into a Muslim continent within several decades only". [11]

---

[10] http://www.dailymail.co.uk/news/article-1324194/Mohammed-popular-baby-boys-ahead-Jack-Harry.html#ixzz13f2fQRNP, Mohammed is now the most popular name for baby boys ahead of Jack and Harry , By JACK DOYLE, 28 October 2010

[11] http://en.wikiquote.org/wiki/Muammar_al-Gaddafi

I shall conclude with what I started: as for the Euro I am not really worried; at most it will slightly change its shape:

- They don`t want you to know: there is no reason for the existence of the Hezbollah.

Hezbollah was established as a militia in 1982 in response to the IDF invasion to Lebanon in June 1982. The IDF invaded Lebanon following the terror attacks on settlements in north Israel. Palestinian terror organizations settled down in southern Lebanon after being expelled from Jordan and they started to attack the northern part of Israel with Katyushka missiles and cannons. The shootings caused the death of Israeli civilians and panic in the settlements in north Israel.

Hezbollah was founded to fight the Israeli presence in Lebanon. It was not the Lebanese government that sought to organize for itself a militia that will act against Israel, but Iran that sent hundreds of officers from the "Revolutionary Guards" to establish the "Hezbollah" movement. The purpose of the movement is to carry out Jihad against the Israeli forces, and if possible to establish, at that opportunity, an Islamic Republic in Lebanon - all the better.

The "Hezbollah" organization was declared as a terror organization by the USA, the EU, Canada, Australia, Bahrain and Israel.

The terror organization is responsible not only for terrorist activity against Israel, but also for worldwide operations against Jews wherever they are and against the Western world. The secretary general of the organization, Hassan Nasrallah, said recently: "If all the Jews gather in Israel, it will save us the need to chase them all over the world".[12]

The various operations of the organization include:

- A terrorist attack at the Israeli Embassy in Buenos Aires on the 17th of March, 1992.
- The bombing of the Jewish Community Center in Buenos Aires on the 18th of July, 1994.
- The kidnapping of Terry Waite, the British priest who was held in captivity for 5 years, chained in a small underground dungeon.

- The kidnapping of Terry Anderson, an American journalist who was held in captivity for 6 and a half years.
- The kidnapping and assassination of the American Colonel William Buckley, Head of the CIA delegation in Lebanon.
- The kidnapping of 3 IDF soldiers on October 2000 and the kidnapping of an Israelis citizen about a week later.
- The kidnapping of 3 IDF soldiers on July 2006.
- Shooting thousands of rockets on communities in north Israel during the second Lebanon war.

---

[12] Source: Wikipedia, "Ideology of Hezbollah."

In 2000 the Israeli government made a decision to withdraw from the security zone in southern Lebanon, a zone that enabled the IDF to defend the north of Israel. The Hezbollah organization took over the area, the members of the organization spread out in the area, they set up outposts and deployed, with the help of Iran and Syria, thousands of rockets and missiles that threaten the whole of Israel.

Since the Hezbollah organization was founded to fight the invasion of the IDF into Lebanon, then after the withdrawal of the IDF the official role of the organizing was over. But the organization is an Iranian front post on the Lebanon-Israel border, and therefore it will naturally find for itself an excuse to continue to exist. Thus, between the borders, on the slopes of Mount Dov, there is an area known as the Shebaa Farm. This area was conquered by Israel from Syria during the six day war. During the IDF`s retreat to the international border, Israel continued to hold it for future negotiations purposes with Syria.

The UN accepted Israel's position and declared that it has completed its retreat from Lebanon, but the Hezbollah continues to consider the Shebba Farm an occupied territory. Otherwise, how can it justify its continued existence?

Currently, huge gas deposits were discovered near the Israeli coasts. A few trillions of cubic   feet. The big drilling, the "Whale" drilling, is considered the world`s largest gas discovery in deep water in the last decade. These discoveries were successful after years of attempts to locate gas and oil in large areas in Israel and the sea nearby. After the discovery of the deposits by the Israeli entrepreneurs, the Lebanese government claimed that these deposits belong to Lebanon as well (the Lebanese government did not bother, of course, to finance the drillings, or any surveys and researches on the subject).

"Naturally", the Hezbollah, that seeks justification for its existence, immediately claimed that the gas deposits belong to him (to Lebanon) [13].

---

[13] Hizbullah: Israel's gas belongs to us, 14/06/ 10 17:41, Adi Ben-Israel and Uzi Blumer ,
http://www.globes.co.il/serveen/globes/docview.asp?did=10005668 74&fid=1725

- They don`t want you to know: missiles are constantly launched toward Israel.

Israel`s area includes about 22,000 square kilometers. Britain`s area includes about 243,000 square kilometers. During World War II about 1,402 rockets were fired on Britain`s cities. London was hit by about 1,358 rockets.[14] Israel, which is less than one-tenth of England, has been hit in the last decade by more than 12,000 rockets (some are called Qassam, some are called Fajr, some are called Katyushka). If you were living in a country that is hit by 12,000 missiles, wouldn`t you demand from your government to stop the shooting of the missiles at any cost?

If so, why when after years of restraint Israel responds to the incessant firing she is accused of committing war crimes?

Operation "Cast Lead" was meant to stop the endless shooting from the Gaza Strip to the "southern" [15] communities of Israel. The operation took place between December 27th 2008 and January 18th 2009. In the Arab world and in the media operation "Cast Lead" was given the vicious name: "The Gaza massacre".

On January 17th, after 22 days of fighting, Israel declared a unilateral cease-fire. 12 hours after that Hamas declared the same.

As a result of the operation, the number of rockets launched on the southern communities of Israel decreased. Yet, each month rockets are fired from the Gaza Strip toward Israel. About 630 kinds of rockets have been fired on Israel from February 2009 until the end of 2010.[16] Does that seem right to you?

The question everyone should ask himself is why does Israel not respond? The answer is rather simple: Operation "Cast Lead" ended with the Goldstone report [17] and an international condemnation of Israel for daring to defend itself.

---

[14] Source, http://en.wikipedia.org/wiki/v-2

[15] Namely a few dozen kilometers from Tel-Aviv

[16] Source: shabak.gov.il

[17] The Goldstone report was formulated by a Committee of Inquiry headed by Richard Goldstone, who was appointed on April 3rd, 2009 by the UN Human Rights Council. The committee's task was to examine the activities of the IDF and the Hamas during Operation "Cast Lead".

The terror organizations that were reinforced by the Operation started slowly and gradually to increase rocket firing from the Gaza Strip. On July 21st 2014, three young boys who were hitchhiking were kidnapped and murdered. The Hamas organization assumed responsibility for the murder. With the increasing shootings and boldness of the terrorist organizations Israel was forced to initiate another operation with the hope to achieve peace in the south. The military operation started on July 8th 2014 and lasted for 50 days.

In the course of the operation, 4,594 rockets and mortar bombs were fired toward Israel, of which 735 were intercepted by the Iron Dome [18], 64 landed in residential areas, 188 failed and fell within the Strip areas and 3,607 landed in open areas.

- They don`t want you to know: in the Israeli "apartheid" Arab citizens enjoy rights such   as they do not have in any Arab country in the world.

I assume that most of you heard the term "apartheid".

I wish to apologize in advance, but it is most likely that the information you have amounts to that "apartheid" existed in South Africa, and now "apartheid" exists in Israel.

So let's put things in order and expose the truth, and nothing but the truth.

The definition of apartheid in Wikipedia is: "The racist policy and racist regime imposed by the white minority Government in South Africa from 1948 until 1990. This policy was based on the principles of racial segregation between white, blacks and colored (mixed) and on granting   privileges to the white minority."

According to the media, apartheid indeed exists in Israel. Otherwise, how is it possible to explain why the "Israeli Apartheid Week" is held every year in different universities around the world?

As part of that event, a whole festival about Israel`s policy is conducted, where the misdeeds of the country which is (incidentally) the only democracy in the Middle East, are displayed, for example: the issue of the "Israeli West Bank barrier" is prominent in that week together with the demand to "demolish the fence".

---

[18] Short range missile defense system.

But what they bother not to tell is that the fence separates between the State of Israel and the "occupied territories", territories from where endless terrorist attacks against Israel came. The "West Bank barrier" managed to minimize the friction, the infiltrations and the terrorist attacks significantly.

The Palestinians in the "occupied territories" live today according to their choice: in the Gaza Strip they chose Hamas that governs them, whereas the West Bank [19] is governed by the Palestinian Authority. If so, it remains to check whether in the boundaries of the State of Israel there is apartheid toward the Arab minority that lives in the country.

---

[19] During reading we shall assimilate a process of rewriting history as is being done all the time. The area called "Judea and Samaria" we shall replace with "The West Bank". Thus we shall also

contribute our share to blurring the connection between the Jewish people and his ancient homeland. An "occupied Palestinian" area cannot be called after Judah - a purely Jewish name!

I present a table summarizing the differences between the apartheid that prevailed in South Africa between1948-1990, and the Israeli "apartheid":

The apartheid regime in South Africa	The apartheid regime in Israel
It is prohibited to vote in the general elections.	Arab citizens vote for the Israeli Knesset.
It is prohibited to be elected in the general elections.	13 Arabs were elected to the 20th Knesset in the elections of 17/03/15.
Black people were forbidden to study in the universities.	Arab citizens are studying in all the universities in Israel.
Black people were not allowed to get medical treatment in hospitals of the white people.	Arab citizens get medical treatment in all the hospitals in Israel.
Black people were forbidden to travel by buses of the white people.	Arab citizens have complete freedom of action like any other Israeli citizen.
Black people were discriminated in all levels of life.	Arab citizens have fully equal rights.
	An Arab judge is serving in the Supreme Court of Israel.
	An Arab girl was elected in 1999 as Miss Israel.

- They don`t want you to know: they admire Hitler and adopt Nazi customs, while referring to Israel`s defense operations as "massacre" and "oppression" and to IDF soldiers – "Nazis".

Hatred for Jews in the Muslim world is mighty and incomprehensible. Jews are presented as the dogs of humanity. The Mufti of Jerusalem, Haj Amin al-Husseini, said: "There is a definite   similarity between the principles of Islam and the principles of Nazism."

The book "Mein Kampf" is a best seller in the region and even in Egypt that has a peace agreement with Israel, "The protocols of the Elders of Zion" [20] appeared in a 14 episodes TV series.

 In TV broadcasts of the Palestinian authority about Jews and Judaism, it is said that the bible of the Jews is a collection of lies about God, his prophets and his words, thus for example: "... they attribute to their prophets the worst crimes: murder, prostitution and drunkenness. The Jews do not believe in God." [21]

Simultaneously, in many mosques Muslims are poisoned by sermons that defame the Jews [22]: "Their tongue never ceases lying, slandering and utter obscenities...The Jews preach permissiveness and corruption, while hiding behind false slogans such as freedom and equality, humanism and brotherhood. They kill Muslim youth, they seduce the woman by disgraceful activities and are active to lure others through her. They contaminate the minds of adults by arousing their lusts. They are jealous of the Muslim woman that hides herself and defends her dignity; that is why they preach to her to expose herself and throw away her values. Their aim   is to destroy the Muslim family, to shatter religious and social foundations. They are cowards in battle. They run for their lives from death and are afraid to fight. They love life.   "Read the history and you will understand that the Jews of yesterday are the forefathers of the worst evil Jews of our time: infidels, distorters of words, worshiping the calf, killers of the prophets, prophecy deniers, scum of the human race, damned by Allah, who turned them into monkeys and pigs. These are the Jews – a constant prolongation of deceit, obstinacy, promiscuity, evil and corruption.

"The Jews are stingy and enslaved to money...Most of the wars in the world, particularly the big modern wars, have been planned and incited by the Jews in order to vandalize the earth and achieve their goals over the ruins of the human race. The Jews are defiled creatures and demonic scum...The Jews are the cause for the suffering of the human race...The Jews are our enemy and hatred to them is ingrained deep in our hearts. A holy war against them is our creed." [23]

---

[20] A blood libel that details the malicious Jewish plan to gain control over the world.

[21] The affinity between Islam and Nazism, Paul Eidelberg and Will Morrissey

[22] The affinity between Islam and Nazism, Paul Eidelberg and Will Morrissey

[23] The affinity between Islam and Nazism, Paul Eidelberg and Will Morrissey.

So how is it possible to make peace with them? And how exactly did Israel turn out to be the bad guy in the story?

MAKES NO SENSE!

Find the differences:

Hezbollah fighters salute with a raised hand [24]

[24] Hezbollah fighters take an oath to continue the path of resistance against Israel during a Hezbollah parade attended by tens of thousands in a Beirut southern suburb Friday, December 22, 2000, on the occasion of "Al-Quds Day" (Jerusalem Day) /AP Archive.

Hitler's book, Mein Kampf, is a best seller in the Arab world:

-They don`t want you to know: the Arab-Israeli conflict is not a dispute over territories.
The conflict is about the very existence of the State of Israel.

Utterances by senior officials and opinion leaders around the world leave no room for doubt: building activities in the settlements constitute an obstacle to peace and a danger to the stabilization of the whole region. As for the present, the exact expression:

"Israeli settlements are an obstacle to peace"

has produced over 129,000 answers in the Google search engine. If I take off the inverted commas, the number exceeds 2,450,000. Among those who thought so were the former UN secretary-General, the French Foreign Minister and the USA Secretary of State. Did anyone stop to ask what exactly this is about? What is the volume of the building activities and why building in the "settlements" constitutes an obstacle to peace, when any negotiation should start from certain base conditions?

The Palestinian demand in managing the negotiation, is that first of all Israel relinquishes building activities in the settlements, acknowledges east Jerusalem as a Palestinian capital, agrees to settle the "refugees" within the State of Israel and in fact bring about the elimination of the State of Israel.

Moreover, is the building of a few hundred residential units- what this is about - is really and truly what constitutes an obstacle to peace? Has Israel not made already several attempts to give them everything (as Bill Clinton said in Camp David in 2000)?

The Palestinians refused without any concession and without conducting any negotiation on their part.

In the end, there is a parallel track: diplomatic moves that allow the Palestinians to obtain Israeli concessions, and on the other hand a track of terrorism that attempts to reach achievements through incessant war of attrition, that includes launching rockets over Israeli cities and attempts to kidnap soldiers.

On the day when the conflict will revolve around the issue of the borders and the partition of territories, it will be quickly resolved. The conflict is not resolved because the Arabs have never given up their intention to destroy the Jewish state, the only democracy in the Middle East.

First it was the Middle Eastern countries that tried to destroy the "imperialistic conqueror" that penetrated "for malicious purposes and to harm" the Arab nation. The "imperialistic conqueror" was so big and cruel, that you may need to use a magnifying glass on order to locate him:

Will you be able to guess where (the hell) the "Despicable Zionist imperialistic entity" is hiding. Among the winners a lottery of an original shirt with the inscription "Boycott Israel" will be drawn.

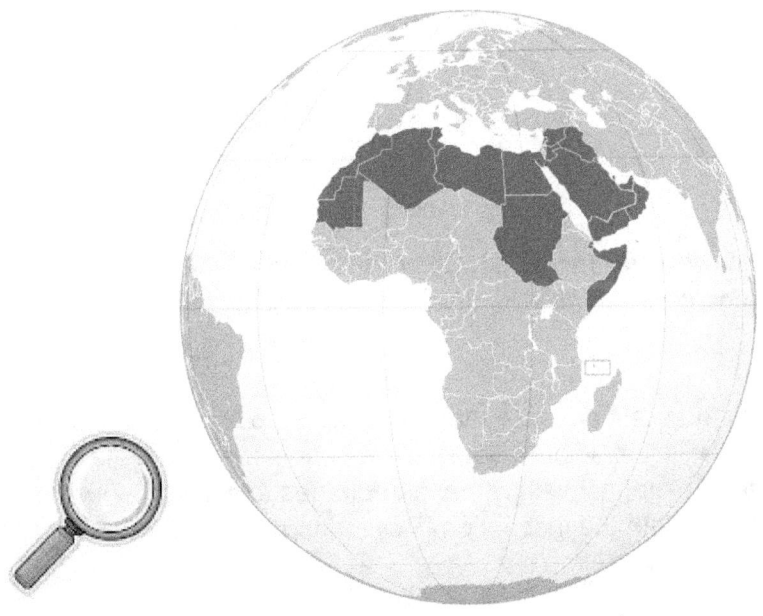

The picture was taken from the entry "The Arab League" in Wikipedia (Author name: Danalm000, 11/11/11). 22 countries are members in the Arab League. Even with a magnifying glass Israel can hardly be seen. Here it is possible to see clearly who the true victim in the story is.

Now see the size of the occupied territories that Israel "occupied" (from whom?)

Source: https://www.cia.gov/library/publications/the-world-factbook/geos/is.html

Notice: how is it possible that the Gaza Strip is an occupied territory if no Israeli/Jew/soldier/Zionist is present in the whole area? A mystery! Here, as well, whoever manages to solve the puzzle will get a shirt with the inscription "Boycott Israel".

- What do they mean when they say occupied territories?

Not a day goes by that the two words "occupied territories" are not mentioned somehow. What exactly are the occupied territories? What is meant, what do you understand?

There is huge gap in the understanding between the Western culture and the Middle Eastern one. For example, the term: "The occupied territories".

The Western listener is convinced that it refers to the West Bank and the Gaza Strip, but the Palestinians refer to the whole region west of the Jordan, namely, the areas of the West Bank, the State of Israel and the Gaza Strip. As far as they are concerned, these are the occupied territories. They never accepted the partition plan of 1947 to divide the country into two states: an Arab state and a Jewish state. They totally deny Israel's right to exist.

For example, currently there is no trace of Israeli rule in the Gaza Strip, nevertheless the Hamas authorities declare openly and through their covenant their wish to annihilate the State of Israel.

For example, most of the West Bank territory is controlled by the Palestinian Authority. Thus, the "occupied territories" are already almost not occupied.

When the Palestinians talk today about occupied territories, they talk about the entire area of the State of Israel and about the dream of the Palestinian to annihilate the only Jewish state in the Middle East by conducting an eternal negotiation and by extorting concessions from Israel. Using the refugee issue as a "justified" solution, aims to eliminate the Jewish essence of Israel by demographic means to.

So the next time someone hears the term "occupied territories" – think again which territories exactly are they talking about.

- Hence, they don`t want you to know: there is no "Palestinian people".

To date, there is no doubt that the Jewish people have existed for thousands of years. I hope that the ferocious incitement and the malicious propaganda will leave this part as a truth, but I doubt it. It is only a matter of time until they will start to doubt that the Jews have existed for such a long time.

I have already come across articles and write-ups that deny the existence of the Jewish people, but this is not what we are discussing right now. The purpose of this book is to assemble and expose some of the falsifications and lies of the formidable propaganda machine, a machine encompassing lands and seas. The propaganda is operating incessantly in order to rewrite history and present the Jews as the worst enemies and thus to outlaw them.

WANTED

Artifacts from "Palestinians Civilization"

$100,000,000
REWARD

Throughout history there has never been a "Palestinian nation." Wherever archaeologists excavate in the holy land, they find no trace of them. Everywhere they find remains of Jewish settlements and of Jewish communities, but not of Palestinian people.

The area on which Israel was established and the whole area on the Western side of the Jordan was called Palestine. This name was adopted by the British who ruled the country during the British

Mandate. The residents of the country were called Palestinians, regardless of their being Arabs or Jews.

Notice that the coin is dated 1942, about 6 years before the Declaration of Independence of the State of Israel. The name "Palestine" is engraved on the coin in 3 languages: Arabic, Hebrew and English. Palestine, meaning the whole region of Israel and its residents whether Arabs or Jews, are all called Palestinians. Notice that in the Hebrew writing of "Palestine", in brackets, two letters are engraved (EI) which are the initials of Eretz Israel. Photo: Istockphoto.

The Roman period in Israel begins in 63 BC, with the conquest of Israel by Pompey, and continues until 324 AD. It is commonly considered as the beginning of the rule of the Byzantine Empire. During this period the name "Palestine" was coined to Israel.

The origin of the name stems from Greek and Latin, and the origin of the name "Palestinians" is based on people called "Philistines" that arrived from Crete [25] and disappeared from History.

On the 2nd of June 1964 the "Palestinian Liberation Organization" was established, headed by Ahmed Shukeiri. A few years earlier, Shukeiri expressed his opinion about the occupied land. On the 31st of May 1956, speaking before the Security Council, he said: "The general opinion is that Palestine is an integral part of Southern Syria".[26]

In one of my other books that deals with the invention of the Palestinian people, I mentioned a paragraph which expresses well the purpose for which the "Palestinian people" was invented in 1964:

This is what Zouheir Mohsen [27] had to say about the "Palestinian people" in an interview he gave to the Dutch newspaper "Troy" on March 1977: "The Palestinian people do not exist. The creation of a Palestinian state is used only as a means in our struggle against Israel for the purpose of our unification as an Arab nation. In today's reality there is no difference between Jordanians, Palestinians, Syrians and Lebanese. We are talking about a "Palestinian people" only for political and tactical purposes since the national Arabic interest requires the principle of the existence of "Palestinian people" in resistance to Zionism....For tactical purposes, Jordan, a sovereign state with defined borders, cannot claim Haifa or Jaffe, while as a Palestinian I can, no doubt, claim Haifa, Jaffe, Beer Sheba and Jerusalem. However, once we set our feet all over Palestine, we will not wait even one minute and unite Palestine and Jordan together". [28]

This part that deals with the creation of the "Palestinian people" is very important in order to understand the lie that became "an indisputable fact", and its acceptance that turned the "Palestinians" into a people of over 12 million people to date. [29]

---

[25] Crete is the fifth largest island in the Mediterranean. In the Bible it is mentioned as the origin of the Philistines. From: Wikipedia under "Crete".

[26] http://www.palestineefacts.org/pf_1948to1967_plo_backgd.php.

(27) Zuheir Mohsen served as Secretary-general (1971-1979) A-Sa'iqa, a Palestinian organization that acted in Syria and was part of the PLO.

(28) From Wikipedia under "Zuheir Mohsen".

(29) https://en.wikipedia.org/wiki/Palestinians.

**- They don`t want you to know: the eternal refugee problem was created by the Arabs
    themselves and by the Arab countries.**

Who would have believed that the "millions" of Palestinian refugees lived not long ago in an area described by the American author Mark Twain as empty deserts, a neglected and abandoned region. Following the War of Independence in 1948 a flux of about 750 thousand Arab refugees left the territory of the State of Israel. These refugees were granted a special status in the United Nation and a relief agency of their own was appointed. This Aid Organization for Palestinian Refugees employs more than 30,000 Palestinians whose pensions have crossed the one billion dollars line.[30]

The definition of the status of these refugees is unique, and it is different from the common "just refugees" definition of the United Nation since the aim of the Aid Organization for Palestinian Refugees is to preserve their status. Being a refugee is a right, a right that is inherited by the grandchildren and even by great-grandchildren thus increasing their number to over 4.7 million.

Generations of "refugees" are sacrificed on the altar of promises by their leaders to return to their land, which was "stolen by the imperialistic conqueror". Many refugees are waiting.

About a million Jewish refugees have been expelled and displaced from their countries, leaving a huge property and lands in areas 3 times bigger than the State of Israel: areas that were stolen from them, that yielded wealth, culture and economic growth to their countries. Magnificent Jewish communities hundreds and thousands of years old have disappeared completely.

Are these the occupied territories? The territories conquered from the Jews?

---

(30) http://www.jha.ac/articles/a135.htm

Israel with its meager resources managed to absorb about a million Jewish refugees, who managed within a few years to integrate, to develop and increase the economy, whereas the issue of the "Palestinian refugees" has not been resolved for over 60 years?

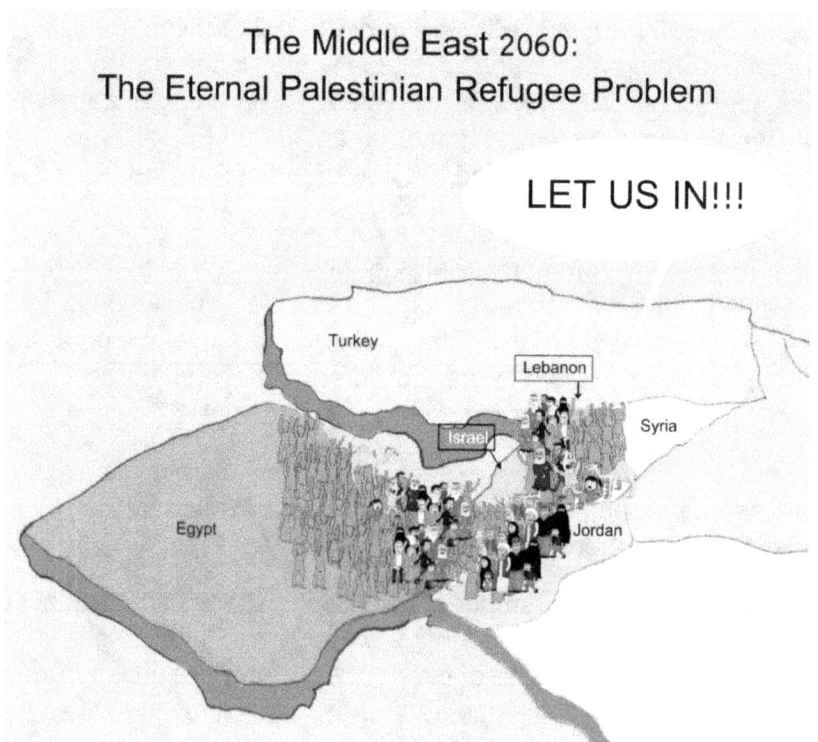

The Palestinian refugees blame Israel for their situation. No one takes responsibility for them. How is it possible that a grandson of a refugee that was born to a father in his country is considered a refugee? Are the grandchildren of World War II refugees who live in the USA considered refugees or Americans? Why does the grandchild of a refugee who has settled in Lebanon over 60 years ago is still considered a Palestinian refugee in Lebanon?

The only reason for that is the intention to preserve their status as "refugees" in order to incorporate them in any future arrangement to absorb them within the State of Israel, and thus to bring about the elimination of its Jewish character and to turn the Jews into a minority in their only country in the world.

The Palestinian Authority is stating repeatedly that any progress with Israel must include also "a just solution to the refugee issue".

Mahmoud Abbas (Abu Mazen) the Chairman of the Palestinian Authority, was quoted on March 1976 in the official newspaper of the Palestinian Liberation Organization in Beirut: "Arab armies entered Palestine in order to protect the Palestinians from Zionist tyranny, but instead they abandoned them, forced them to immigrate and leave their country, and threw them into prisons that resemble the ghettos in which the Jews lived." [31]

[31] http://israelipalestinian.procon.org/view.answers.php?questionID=481, Ian J. Bickerton, PhD, Associate Professor of Middle Eastern and United States History at the University of New South Wales-Australia, and Carla L. Klausner, PhD, Professor of Modern Middle East, Medieval Europe and Judaic Studies at the University of Missouri-Kansas City, in their 2002 book A Concise History of the Arab-Israeli Conflict

Abu-Mazen, who is considered the "moderate" partner, puts the responsibility for the problem of the Palestine refugees on the Arab armies. The responsibility lies with the Arab countries, and it is fitting that they should bear the responsibility for dealing with the problem.

Nevertheless, in every speech Abu Mazen mentions the inclusion of the "right of return" as a basic condition to any arrangement.

And hence we will check who that "partner" for peace is?

In 1982 Mahmud Abbas (Abu Mazen) finished his PhD studies in History in the USSR in a University named after Patrice Lumumba. His PhD thesis: "The connections between Nazism and Zionism, in the years 1933-1945", was written in Russian. His thesis was the basis for a book he wrote in Arabic called: "The other aspect: the secret connections between the Nazis and the leadership of the Zionist movement". Abbas claimed in the book that the Zionist movement collaborated with the Nazis in exterminating the Jewish people, in exchange for signing the "transfer agreement" between Nazi Germany and the Jewish Agency. Under the agreement the transfer of the property of tens of thousands of Jews from Germany to Israel was allowed. [32]

So no wonder they don`t want you to know what is broadcasted on the Palestinian television:

Television, besides it being a cheap entertainment for the masses, possesses the ability to transfer visually and vocally messages to the wide public, and to shape its opinion according to the marketed agenda.

The agenda that is incessantly brutally marketed does not offer any future or hope for peace and brotherhood among the nations. The Palestinian media, and in this context also the Arab media, nurtures anti-Semitism, nourishes it, chews it and serves it on a golden platter to the hungry minds of its viewers.

Children grow up in hate, watching from infancy "educational" programs, in which children their age are interviewed on television and express their wish to fulfill themselves in the future as Shahid. This is what they are watching, on this is they are educated.

----

(32) From Wikipedia under: "Mahmud Abbas"

(The photo is taken from the Hamas Al Aqsa channel, September 22 2009, courtesy of the Palestinian (Media Watch – www.palwatch.org)

Do they want peace?

MAKES NO SENSE!

It is not only the media that perpetuates the conflict and the hatred for Jews. The Palestinian education system contributes to it a lot.

A wild anti-Semitic incitement occurs in the Palestinian schools, the hatred is fostered in the pages of the textbooks. Facts are replaced with lies and demonization is performed constantly in the education system that formulates the next generation of Palestinians. According to the educational programs, a generation will grow that will see Jihad as a way of life and non-recognition in the State of Israel - a fact. Denial of the holocaust is fait accompli. The hatred for the Jews is burning. The solution is the annihilation of the Jewish state that is built on large portions of the historic Palestine. Schools are named after Israeli towns, streets are named after terrorists.

- They don`t want you to know: everyone is a Palestinian.

Unlike other nations, in which people are born into a cohesive and known identity such as the British, French, American etc. a significant part of the Palestinians become Palestinians even if they were not born as such. For example: Yasser Arafat, the former Chairman of the Palestinian Authority was not born a Palestinian, but he simply turned it into a career. In many of the refugee camps, some of the refugees managed to leave (to the dissatisfaction of UNRWA [33]) and to stop being refugees. The desertions created a vacuum that was filled by settlers from the region that got an opportunity to improve their lives. The refugee camps are settlements for all intents and do not resemble real refugee camps such as in Africa. Thus hundreds of thousands Palestinians pop up out of nowhere, and they are still going strong.

---

[33] A reminder: the UNRWA - United Nations Relief and Works Agency for Palestine Refugees. An agency devoted entirely to the problem of the Palestinian refugees. A solution for the rest of the refugees around the world is through the UN Commission for Refugees - UNHCR

- They don't want you to know what the political platform of the Hamas is.

Although the Hamas organization has been declared as a terrorist organization, sometimes squeaks are heard by all sorts of politicians and activists calling for a dialogue with Hamas. That is logical - you make peace with enemies, no?

Most of the conflicts between countries are rooted in the control over territories, resources, sources of energy or food. But here, in the Middle East, the rules are a bit different.

The Hamas, as part of the "Muslim Brotherhood" organization, declare in the "Hamas Covenant" that the source of the conflict is religious. As far as they are concerned, it is essential to observe the Islamic commandments and to start a Jihad against the Jews, and not only against the Jews but also against the heretics, namely, anyone who is not a Muslim. This is a divine imperative!

Already from the introduction to the Hamas Covenant it can be understood that peace with Hamas will happen long after E.T. will land here: "Israel will continue to exist until Islam wipes it out, the same way it wiped out whatever preceded it".

Article 8 in the covenant defines the goal of the Hamas movement: Allah is its purpose, the Prophet is its paragon, the Koran is its constitution, the Jihad is the route and death for the sake of Allah is its sublime desire.

And what about "peace"? Someone forgot to insert it!

Article 11 deals with the occupied territories. Many tend to regard the occupied territories as territories held by Israel by force, i.e., the Gaza Strip, from which Israel withdrew in the summer of 2005, the West Bank, most of which is governed by the Palestinian Authority.

But as far as the Hamas is concerned, the occupied territory is the whole area west of Jordan including Israel and the "occupied territories". Later on in article 11 it seems that an occupied territory is any territory that has once been an Islamic territory.

Following are large portions of the article: The resistance movement believes that the land of Palestinian is a Muslim Waqf, for generations of Muslims till doomsday arrives (Palestine is all the land west of Jordan). It, or any part of it, must not be neglected or conceded.

It is important to note: This is a law in the Islamic Shari'a, a law like any law that applies to any country conquered by force by the Muslims, since during the occupation the Muslims dedicated these countries to generations of Muslims till doomsday!

Maybe there is some hope after all. For example: What does article 13 in the Hamas covenant have to tell us: "Initiatives and what is called peace solutions and international conferences, contradict the principles of the Islamic Resistance Movement....These conferences are nothing more than a way to perpetuate the hold of the heretics in the land of the Muslims as arbitrators ....There is no solution to the Palestinian question but in Jihad. Initiatives, propositions and international conferences, are all a waste of time, nonsense and futile."

Let's continue to article 20: "Jewish Nazism included women and children and intimidation campaigns of the public. They damage the livelihood of people, extort their money and threaten their dignity. They treat people as if they were the most despicable war criminals. Exile from a homeland is a kind of murder" (I wonder what my mother and father would say and another million Jewish refugees that were deported from their homeland).

The classic anti-Semitism and the "scapegoat syndrome", as well, are not absent from   the covenant.

Here is article 22:

"They have diligently accumulated enormous wealth and influence which they used to realize their dream. With their money they managed to control the international media, newspapers, news agencies and publication houses, broadcasting station etc.

Using their money they have created revolutions in the world in order to materialize   their interests and pick up the fruits. They were behind the French Revolution, the Communist Revolution and most of the revolutions in the world. (Author's note: Is the "Arab Spring" also such a revolution?) Using their money they managed to gain control over many countries while they looted their treasures and spread their corruption all over. They were behind World War I, when they managed to destroy the Islamic Caliphate state. They derived material profits and gained control over many sources of wealth. (Author's note: Did they also initiate World War II? Did they initiate their own destruction?) They founded the League of Nations through which they ruled the world. They were behind World War II and derived huge profits from arms trade and strove to establish their own country. They initiated the establishment of the United Nation and the Security Council in order to be able to continue to rule the world. No war is conducted without their involvement".

Peace will come only in a single situation:

"The day the Arabs will put down their weapons there will be peace".

(The rest of the sentence, you already know).

- They do not want you to know: there is an Islamic Imperialism [34]

The Zionist entity is described by the propaganda as the representative of Western Imperialism that has established in the heart of the Arab nation an imperialistic outpost. Iran leader said many times that the existence of the Zionist entity is possible only due to the support of Western imperialism. Deportation (at best) and destruction of the "Zionist entity" are moral imperatives that Islam must perform in order to correct the historic injustice. This is an example of how the victim turns out into a criminal. While the spotlights are aimed at the "Zionist entity", the number-one export industry in the world today: the export of Islam is operating quietly and undisturbed.

Quietly, countries are conquered by Islam. The massive immigration and the high rate of fertility change the demographics of the countries, so that in a few years their original character will disappear and their turning into another Muslim country will be only a matter of time. Europe is conquered by masses from the Islamic army. Democratic European countries are trying to stop the drift, but as always, when it comes to do with Europe – it is too slow and too late.

---

[34] Imperialism is gaining control by one country over other countries and nations and exploiting their resources in order to increase its own power and wealth.

"Estimates show that in 2010 between 20 to 25% of the population in Amsterdam, Brussels and Marseille, were Muslims (my attempts to obtain more updated information failed – I wonder why?!). It is estimated that the Muslim population in Birmingham, Cologne, Copenhagen, Leicester, London, Paris, Rotterdam, Stockholm, Strasbourg and Hague, is between 10% and 20%. In Antwerp, Berlin, Hamburg and Vienna the Muslim population is estimated between 5%-10%". (35)

The only imperialism that exists in the world today is the Islamic imperialism. Soon, Europe will join to the territorial contiguous of the Islamic nation, from Indonesia in the east to the British Islamic Republic. In the American continent as well the phenomenon exists, all the more forcefully in Canada. Africa has been already conquered by the Islamic imperialism.

- They don`t want you to know: the goal of Islam is to rule the world.

In February 2011 a coup occurred in Egypt. The era of dictatorship ended and the democratic era began. This opinion is shared by journalists, commentators and the media in all its forms. It is time to give the millions of youngsters a more promising future, it is time to allow them to live a democratic life, to make it possible for them to criticize, to express their opinion and make a decent living. To a large extent, this was also the situation on the eve of the Hamas takeover of the Gaza Strip. Then, as well, "democratic" elections were held, and in a democratic way, the people in the Gaza Strip elected Hamas (and they live peacefully and tenderly ever since).

For those who live thousands of kilometers away from this region the process may seem welcome. A coup in Egypt that ends with the establishment of a democratic entity. But allow me to be skeptical. Since the coup the "Muslim Brotherhood" came to power.

---

(35) http://www.hudson-ny.org/1536/islam-religion-of-europe, Will Islam Become the Religion of Europe? by Soeren Kern, September 9, 2010

After a few months there was another revolution against the coup of the coup and the army returned to power. The "Muslim Brotherhood" managed, for a short period, to achieve their goal. In fact, the "Muslim Brotherhood" managed eventually to be elected in a democratic way to govern Egypt and represent a segment of the population that has been oppressed so far. According to Wikipedia, the movement of the "Muslim Brotherhood" is a popular Muslim Sunni religious movement, with a political affiliation to Islam. The "Muslim Brotherhood" was founded in Egypt in 1928 by Imam al-Banna after the collapse of the Ottoman Empire. Its members aspire to impose the Islam religion in the constitution and in social life, by turning Egypt and the other Arab countries into countries governed by religion, with all their systems operating subject to the laws of the Sharia. The motto of the movement is "Islam is the solution".

The "Muslim Brotherhood" movement has branches in 70 countries. The members of the movement have declared over the years that they participated in most of the conflicts connected with Islam, beginning with the Israel-Arab wars, Algeria's War of Independence and the recent conflicts in Afghanistan and in Kashmir.

The "Muslim Brotherhood" in Egypt is a popular organization, and its name was mentioned in connection with underground political activities, including active participation in the demonstrations in Egypt, which led to the end of the reign of President Hosni Mubarak. In other countries the local organizations of the movement have more prominent roles and even seats in parliament. Members of the movement supported or led to the establishment of various organizations, such as the Islamic movement and the Islamic Jihad in Egypt, and the movement of the Islamic communities called "Mujahideen" in Europe and in the United States.

It is worth noting: the "Muslim Brotherhood" has branches in 70 countries. The motto of the movement is "Islam is the solution". What does it mean? Mahdi Akef, Head of the movement made it perfectly clear in his speech of the 22nd of February 2007: [36]

"The Jihad will lead to the shattering of Western civilization and will replace it with Islam, that will rule the world."

Moreover, Akef stated that in case the Muslims will be unable to achieve this goal in the near future, "the Muslims must continue the Jihad which will cause the collapse of Western civilization and the rise of the Islamic culture on its ruins".

How is it possible to promote this idea?

_____

(36) THE MUSLIM BROTHERHOOD'S PROPAGANDA OFFENSIVE, by Dr. Rachel Ehrenfeld and Alyssa A. Lappen,   02-Apr-07
http://www.acdemocracy.org/viewarticle.cfm?id=344

The "Muslim Brotherhood" movement wrote a document titled: "The establishment of the Islamic government" that details the specific instructions for its achievement. These instructions include:

"The preparation of society is achieved by programs aimed at disseminating the Islamic culture using the different communications media, mosques, urging others to convert to Islam, work in public organizations such as syndicates, parliaments, students unions."

And what does the Western world have to say about that? After the ouster of the Egyptian president Hosni Mubarak, the USA Secretary of State said:

"The United States will be happy to conduct a dialog with the "Muslim Brotherhood" movement". [37]

Talking is never a bad thing.

It can be felt well in Europe, it can be felt in Africa and it can be felt in other places, such as Canada and in the largest heretics` stronghold, which is the "Great Satan".

It is happening right now in your house, don`t say you didn`t know!

The kind of posters that are shown in almost every demonstration or parade (AFP PHOTO / Martyn Wheatley)

(37)   http://articles.cnn.com/2011-06-
30/world/egypt.muslim.brotherhood.us_1_muslim-brotherhood-freedom-
and-justice-party-egypt?_s=PM:WORLD

- What are the Sharia laws that will apply once the Islam gains control over the world?

The Sharia is the Islamic religious law that regulates all spheres of life and of society. Heavy penalties are due to those who break the law: amputation of limbs for thieves, stoning to death of adulterers, death penalty for whoever converts and an abundance of   other progressive laws. Countries such as Iran or Saudi Arabia follow the Sharia laws.

For example: the dress code for women includes exposure of the eyes only.

Although there are many interpretations of the Sharia and different perspectives, it is agreed among the Muslims that the Sharia is a reflection of God's will for humanity. The Sharia must be in the purest sense, perfect and unchangeable. The development of the Sharia is an effort to reflect in a more perfect way God's will. [38]

Well, so it exists and it happens, who cares? After all it is implemented in Saudi Arabia and Iran and it does not really interest the Western person.

I suppose that some of you think that it is about just a few fanatics, but it is worth remembering that a considerable part of history was outlined by a crazy person or by a group of lunatics.

Superficially, the matter seems light years away. If you think so as well – you are wrong. See for example the first signs in Britain:

Islamic extremists called on the Muslims in Britain to establish three independent states within Britain.

Under the caption "Muslims must establish Islamic emirates in Britain", "this is the right time to proclaim the areas with a large

Muslim population as emirates, where the Muslims will live according to the Sharia as much as possible with courts of their own, community policing, schools and even trading." [39]

So we don`t panic too much, the media makes sure to soften the event. They clarify that these are not "just" Islamic activists but "extreme" activists. Like that it is perceived better, less threatening, more politically correct: that same politically correctness that destroys all that is good.

———————

[38] From Wikipedia under "Sharia"

[39] http://www.dailymail.co.uk/news/article-2011433/Islamic-extremists-set-independent-states-UK-fall-Shariah-law.htm

And by the way, if by any chance you are Western citizens, make sure to avoid getting into neighborhoods where the following posters appear:

This kind of posters are propagated in about 12 cities in England. In these cities whole areas are subjected to the Sharia laws and are considered outside the jurisdiction of Britain. This phenomenon spreads out in many European countries such as France, Belgium, Germany, Sweden and the Netherlands.

- They don`t want you to know that as far as they are concerned all of you are heretics: you are next in line!

From the article "Jihad today" by Prof. Menachem Milson: [40]

Jihad is the religious duty of every Muslim. The term jihad refers to 3 aspects in the life of a Muslim: the first is the internal struggle to keep the faith, the second is the struggle to improve Muslim society, and the third is a struggle through a holy war.

According to the traditional Islamic dogma, Allah destined the Muslims to be victorious and to reach the status of superiority over the other religions in the world. Allah validated the message of Islam in the military victory he bestowed on the Muslims under the leadership of Muhammad in the battle of Badr. It was during the month of Ramadan in 624. In the battle of Badr 300 Muslim soldiers, led by Muhammad, defeated the army of the Quraysh tribe that numbered 950 men. In Muslim consciousness the battle of Badr has the status of a formative event.

This victory was not a single victory; it was followed by many victories, and following them the Islamic Empire that ruled from India to the Atlantic Ocean, was founded. Thus, the sense of superiority and of victory became an element in the collective identity of the Muslims. "The Islam is superior and no one can surpass it" – this saying is attributed to the Prophet Muhammad and it reflects the Muslim sense of superiority. This self-image of the Muslims – even when it ceased to be based on political and military reality – was not undermined for many centuries.

According to the traditional Islamic dogma, human beings are divided into two – the believers in Islam, called "believers", and all the non-Muslims, called "heretics". The only true religion is - the Islam; the Muslims are commanded to spread Islam all over the world and the Jihad is the means for that.

Islam distinguishes in the crowd of heretics between two main groups – the heathens and the "scholars" – Ahal al-Katav, the Jews and Christians. Islam acknowledges that in the past the Jews and the Christians were granted a divine revelation and laws that were given from heaven, but they falsified the words of God and the book they got from heaven and therefore they are heretics.

---

(40) The full article appears in the Memri website:

http://www.memri.org.il/cgi-webaxy/sal/sal.pl?act=show&ID=107345_memri&lang=he&dbid=articles&dataid=11

The heathens have one choice: to accept the religion of Islam, or to die, as is said in the Quran: "After the holy months come to an end, you should kill the mushrikun (namely the polytheists) wherever you find them, catch them and besiege them and ambush them everywhere...." The verse that instructs this (Quran, Surah 9, verse 5) is called "The Verse of Swords".

"The scholars" Ahel al-Kitav, are entitled to a special status and their fate is different from the fate of the heathen heretics. The Muslims are commanded to fight then until they accept Islam, or alternatively, agree to pay a poll tax called "G'zihn". This law is based on the words of the Quran: "Fight the people who do not believe in Allah and not on the last day and they do not forbid what Allah and his messenger have forbidden, and who do not uphold the true faith – those of them who were given the book – until they pay the G'zihn with their own hands while they are humiliated". This verse (Quran, Surah 9 verse 29), which defines in principle the attitude toward the "scholars", is called   in Muslim literature Aait al-G'zihn ("The verse of the poll tax"). The payment of the poll tax indicates, among others, the submission to Muslim rule and the acceptance of the status of protégés, called in Arabic Aahal al-Dama.

Just as people are divided into two kinds - Muslims and heretics, thus the world is divided into two kinds – Dar al-Islam, namely "The house of Islam" - the countries that are ruled by Muslims, and Dar al-harb, 'The house of war", namely all the countries that are not under Muslim rule and that must be conquered by the force of arms, meaning by Jihad.

- When talking about occupied territories, does it mean also Spain?

Pursuant to the previous part, the planet on which we exist and some of us also live, is divided into two, according to Islam: Dar al-Islam – the countries that are ruled by Muslims, and Dar al-harb – the countries that are not under Muslim rule and that must be conquered by the means of Jihad.

An example for countries that are defined Dar al-harb – is to be found in the European continent. That same continent that ejected its Jews, absorbs "with pleasure" an endless stream of Muslim immigrants. An example for the European hypocrisy is Spain. Spain was known for its brutal inquisition [41] that was tested on many Jews. This is the same Spain where indictments were submitted against Israeli officers and senior leaders who were charged with committing war crimes against the "Palestinian people".

But the area known as "Spain" is occupied to exactly the same extent as Israel was occupied by the "Zionists". The territory of Spain is a Muslim territory conquered by the heretics. It is just a matter of time until the area will return to be Muslim again, as it should be:

"Islamic lands occupied by the enemy will become Islamic again. Moreover, we will reach beyond these countries that were lost at some point. We declare that we will conquer Rome, as Constantinople was conquered in the past, and will be conquered again." [42]

---

[41] The inquisition was established in the 13th century by the Catholic Church headed by Pope Gregory IX. The inquisition was awarded powers of investigation which enabled to fight Christian sects that were getting common at the time. The Spanish inquisition, that was established on November 1st 1478 by a proclamation from Pope Sixtus IV, was aimed

primarily against the Jews. Many Jews, at that time, were forced to convert to Christianity or get killed. The inquisition used cruel inquiry methods against these converted Jews in order to make them admit that their conversion was for the sake of appearance. Later on these Jews were taken to the gallows and were burned alive. Author's note: Today, many Museums of Torture are spread across Europe where one can visit for amusement purposes and watch the torture facilities that definitely did not amuse those who experienced them.

(42)

http://www.catholic.org/international/international_story.php?id=27930

For a more profound understanding of the Middle East I would like to refer you to the series of books I wrote on this subject.

You could find them under my name Kobi Shashoua on Amazon or on:

www.kobisha.com

You are welcome to contact me directly through my e-mail:

kobimnsil@gmail.com

Tel: 972-54-8030648

Your truly,

Kobi Shashoua

A must book to anyone who lives in a democratic country. "The Spring of nations", that was perceived with a naïve hope by Western governments was no more than a preface to the atrocities that took shape across nations and continents. This time, as well, the West is perceived in its naivety or its arrogance as if trying to understand simply and superficially the origin of the ancient conflict that is taking place in the depth of Islam. Again the West is caught unprepared, astounded by the truth it refuses to accept. In this book I will expose the reader to this truth that is recited in mosques, in sermons and out aloud in the Islamic street. Every person must be aware of this truth because the danger is increasing and is carried by the endless flows of refugees that stream into the democratic world.

Kobi Shashoua is an author and lecturer. He wrote the most comprehensive book to date regarding the Israeli-Palestinian conflict, "Israel: the truth, the whole truth and nothing but the truth." This book leads the reader chapter after chapter through the complex reality of the conflict and dissects the reasons for the crisis, it reveals to the reader the true faces of the parties involved, presents the tactics, the strategies and the real goals, those that lie underneath the surface. The author also wrote the book series "Facts you must know about the Middle East." The book you are holding now is from that series.

The author, who lives in Israel, the most dangerous neighborhood in the world in the heart of the Middle East, shares with us the facts together with the unique insights and understanding of the region where he lives. We welcome you to participate in this journey from a safe distance.